Samsung Galaxy Note 8

Get the Most Out Of Your Device - Explore Ultimate Tips and Tricks

written by David F. Johnson

Table of Contents

INTRODUCTION

Samsung's camp is abuzz with activity, with the imminent launch of the next-generation Samsung Galaxy Note 8. There are many exciting rumors floating around the internet that the Samsung Galaxy Note8 is poised to potentially change the smartphone game and bring it to the next level. In this guide, we take a look at all the buzzes surrounding the many features of the premium smartphone from Samsung.

SAMSUNG GALAXY NOTE8 REVIEW

The new Samsung Galaxy Note8 is by far the largest screened smart phone to be released by Samsung and sets a new precedent in the market by almost crossing over to the tablet form of an iPad 2 or Samsung Galaxy Tab.

Big and powerful, the Samsung Galaxy Note 8 is made for smartphone enthusiasts and power users. It stands out with being Samsung's first dual-camera phone, enabling real 2x zoom and background blur effects. It is also the first Galaxy Note device built around the newer 18.5:9 display aspect ratio, which allows it to fit a huge, 6.3-inch display in a body not impossible to handle. The S-Pen — a trademark feature for the Note series — is now more precise and more useful with more features built around it. And no less importantly, the phone is built to higher safety standards than its predecessor.

The Samsung Galaxy Note offers decent levels of storage, with 64GB versions available. This means that all your files will fit comfortably in the phone, be they music tracks, videos, work files, photo or applications which have been downloaded from the Android Market. As if this wasn't enough, a further 53GB of storage can be attained by utilising the built in microSD card slot.

Those of you who regularly browse the internet will surely appreciate the data download speeds that the Samsung Galaxy Note8 is capable of. When a Wi-Fi signal is not accessible, the phone utilised the 3G coverage whereby an HSDPA connection can provide download speeds more than 21 Mbps, which is currently the fastest achievable speed on a smartphone.

The Samsung Galaxy Note8 comes pre-loaded with the latest Android 7.1 operating system. On the reverse of the Galaxy Note is an 12 mega pixel camera which allows for video capture at full 1080p HD quality and on the front of the phone is a 8 mega pixel camera for video calls, Samsung is taking users through the features of its dual camera. It starts by comparing it to the iPhone 7, suggesting the phone will offer superior image stablisation than its Apple rival. The Note 8 will also offer "Dual Capture", taking depth effects even further. Note 8 users will be able to live focus pictures, fading out the background in real time, this is a very high specification handset packing some of the latest technology and features hence the price tag is likely to stay above many other models for some time.

FEATURES AND SPECIFICATIONS
Design
The Galaxy Note8 is designed for you to use with ease and simplicity. The beautiful curves and seamless body are engineered to offer you a comfortable grip and more space for you to write freely with the S Pen. The fingerprint scanner is virtually flush with the back, and the Home button is embedded underneath the Infinity Display to stay invisible until you need it. It's the beginning of a seamless experience.

Display

The innovation of the Galaxy Note8's design makes possible the 6.3" Infinity Display. It's the biggest ever for a Galaxy Note. Even watching movies is simply more enjoyable with the Infinity Display's 18.5:9 aspect ratio. In landscape mode, the Galaxy Note8 offers a 14% wider viewing area that makes for a richer, more immersive experience that pulls you in wherever you are.

Pressure-sensitive feature

Samsung has managed to integrate pressure sensitive technology into the Galaxy Note 8's huge 6.4-inch display.The pressure sensitive technology works similar to Apple's 3D Touch display released with its iPhone 7. This will enable users to apply different levels of pressure to the display to toggle new functionality. It isn't out of the ordinary to see Samsung following Apple's footsteps. It has been known to do it ✦uite well given its past records.

✳ Camera

Samsung's Galaxy Note 8 is a giant phone with a ton of features, but one of its most prominent ones is its new dual-camera setup. This system, which includes two 12-megapixel cameras with different focal length lenses, lets you take either wide-angle or zoomed-in pictures.

TheNote 8's camera also lets you mimic the blurred background that you can get with a larger, DSLR camera. This can be cool for portraits, close-ups, or anything else where you want your subject to stand out from the background as much as possible.

2x optical zoom + dual OIS

Take crisp and clear shots with the Galaxy Note8's dual camera. It supports 2x optical zoom to let you zoom in clearly. And both cameras have optical image stabilization (OIS) to produce photos that come out beautifully steady even with camera shake.

Live focus

Get the focus you want before you press the shutter button. Live focus lets you take beautiful bokeh shots where you make your subject stand out. And if you're not entirely satisfied, you always have the option to adjust the level of background blur afterwards.

Dual Capture

While you're focused on taking a Live focus photo, Dual Capture photographs what's happening outside the frame. That way you get to enjoy the moments you might have otherwise missed.

Low light camera

Great photos are just a snap away even when it's dark. The Galaxy Note8's wide-angle camera captures more light with its large 1.4μm pixels and bright F1.7 lens, while focusing fast and accurately thanks to the Dual Pixel Sensor.

Front camera

Flip to the front camera to take a selfie or group shot you'd be more than happy to share. Its bright lens keeps details clear even in low light, while Smart Auto Focus tracks the faces in the shot.

RAM

The Galaxy Note 8 is the world's first ever smartphone to ship with 6GB of RAM. The fact that the Note 8 feature a better RAM more than its predecessor, could indicate Samsung has some pretty big plans for the device. Rumors say that the Note 8 is a laptop hybrid and a smartphone.

Battery

Earlier this year, rumors popped up about the Samsung Galaxy Note 8 potentially packing a mammoth 4000 mAh battery. The battery in the Note 8 is "only" 3,330 mAh - simply huge - and is also non-removable. Rapid charging and wireless charging technology are also supported on the phone.

Storage

The phone come with three different internal storage variants: 64GB, 128GB and 256GB. Samsung Galaxy can offer a lot of storage and probably do so at a reduced cost. Indeed the company is offering a free 128GB Samsung branded microSD card as a pre-order benefit for the Note 8.

Key Features
- 6.3-inch screen Super AMOLED display

- Wireless charging

- Water resistance

- Fingerprint sensor (on the back)

- 3,330 mAh battery

- 6 GB of RAM

- 64/128/256 GB of internal storage, which is expandable with a memory card

- Adreno 540 Graphics

- Octa-core, 2350 MHz, Kryo 280, 64-bit, 10 nm processor

- Built-in (Qi, Powermat)Wireless charging

- DLNA, Wireless screen share, SlimPort Screen mirroring

- Earpiece, Loudspeaker

- Accelerometer, Gyroscope, Compass, Hall (for flip covers), Barometer. Sensors

- 6.40 x 2.94 x 0.34 inches (162.5 x 74.8 x 8.6 mm). Dimensions

- 6.88 oz (195 g) Weight

TOP TIPS AND TRICKS

As one of the best and most praised smartphones released in 2017, the Samsung Galaxy Note 8 continues to gain traction even today. We've seen it everywhere online, where people ask all kinds of questions on how to make the best of this device.

Sit back and relax because you have gotten the best guide that will unveil the various tips and tracks for Samsung Galaxy Note 8 might as well be considered the ultimate guide in terms of user experience. To show you what to expect, bear in mind that the information from below will be divided into 5 main categories:

1. Security and privacy related questions: fingerprint sensor, SIM unlock, block calls, delete browser history, find lost Samsung Galaxy Note 8;

2. Efficiency questions: how to remove bloatware, how to handle slow Internet, and how to work with the Private Mode on Samsung Galaxy Note 8;

3. Customization options: change Lock Screen, change style and font, set custom ringtones on Samsung Galaxy Note 8;

4. Unique uses and instructions: Wi-Fi printing, TV wireless connection, flashlight activation, alarm clock configuration on Samsung Galaxy Note 8;

5. Special features: make it read texts, deactivate S Voice, work with Autocorrect, create new folders on Samsung Galaxy Note 8

SECURITY & PRIVACY
How to activate and configure the Fingerprint Sensor on Samsung Galaxy Note 8:

• Go to Settings

- Access Lock Screen & Security

- Tap on Fingerprint

- Select Add fingerprint

- Follow the prompts, until the fingerprint is 100% scanned

- Set up a backup password

- Enable Fingerprint Lock

- Confirm with OK

- Leave the menus and test to see how it is to unlock the device by simply holding the finger on the home button!

With this built-in fingerprint scanner, you can forget about patterns and passwords. The latter was set during the configuration process only as an emergency solution

How to unlock the SIM of your Samsung Galaxy Note 8:
- Contact the customer helpline of your cellular company

- Ask for the Note 8 unlock code

- Provide the IMEI number to confirm that you are the owner

- Wait to receive the code via email.

This option is essential when you are traveling abroad and you want to be able to use a different SIM with your smartphone to reduce the voice costs. Just remember that it might take a few days until you will receive the code on the email, so you'd better plan in advance!

How to block a particular number from calling your Samsung Galaxy Note 8:

- Launch the Phone app

- Switch to the Call Log

- Tap on the number you want to block, from the recent calls' history

- Tap on the MORE option

- Tap on "Add to auto reject list".

How to delete the browser history on your Samsung Galaxy Note 8:

•   Launch the Android browser whose history you want to delete

•   Tap the three-dot symbol to access its menu

•   Tap the Settings option

•   Tap the Privacy option

•   Find the Delete Personal Data entry

•   Select the types of data that you want to delete – navigation history, password details, auto-fill information, cache, cookies etc

•   Tap on Delete;

Wait for it to finish and continue your navigation with a clear browsing history.

How to find or deal with a lost/stolen Samsung Galaxy Note 8:

•   First of all, you must have some tools installed on it so you can locate the device and secure it remotely when you lose access to it

- The best tools that users have at hand are the Android Device Manager and the Lookout

- For remote data access, AirDroid is a very popular app that can help you control even the camera access and your SMS text archive

- As soon as you get your Samsung Galaxy Note 8 back, make sure you take extra protection measures like the ones suggested above!

EFFICIENCY

How to remove the bloatware from your Samsung Galaxy Note 8:

- Go to the App drawer

- Tap on the Edit button

- You'll see that most apps will get a Minus icon next to their names

- This means that you can uninstall or disable those apps

- Tap the minus icon for each of the apps you want to remove.

You'll notice that apps like the ones from the Google suite (Gmail, Play Store, Google+ etc.) can be easily downloaded, just like the ones from the Samsung's S Health suite, S Voice etc. But there are also apps that you cannot remove because their absence might affect the system performances.

All in all, most of that bloatware can be eliminated and it appears that the South Korean law dictated this way. The goal is to give users as much freedom in personalizing their devices as possible.

How to handle the slow Internet issue on Samsung Galaxy Note 8:
- Swipe down from the top of the screen

- Access the Settings menu

- Go to Connections

- Tap on Wi-Fi

- Turn off the Wi-Fi by tapping the slider next to it.

The reason why we have recommended you to do the entire above is simple – in most of the situations, the Samsung Galaxy Note 8 remained stuck on a very weak Wi-

Fi signal. When you force it to stay on mobile data alone or connect it to a different wireless network, the internet speed should be visibly accelerated.

The essentials of how to use the Private Mode on Samsung Note 8:

The Private Mode is one of the coolest protection measures that Note 8 users have at hand. It's a built-in feature, so you don't have to install any other third-party app, and it has a rapid command that you can try with the tap of a finger.

When the Private Mode is active, you can see photos, videos, and other files that are invisible in the normal running mode. That's when you can add new content to your Secure Folder and when you can access sensitive information. Once you disable the feature, the data becomes suddenly invisible, though, it still remains on your smartphone.

Both the activation and the deactivation of this mode can be done from the extended menu that shows up when you swipe down from the top of the display. The Private Mode has its own icon in there and suffices to touch it – you'll be asked to use your password code or the unlock pattern that you have selected the first time when you activate it and you'll gain access. To deactivate the Private Mode, it's even easier because you just have to swipe downward again and tap the icon once.

CUSTOMIZATION

How to set up a custom Lock Screen on your Samsung Galaxy Note 8:

• Go to the Home screen main panel

• Find an empty spot

• Tap and hold on that spot

• When the Edit Mode launches, release your tap

• Look at the bottom of the screen for the options listed in there

• You'll find the icons labeled as Widgets, Wallpaper, and Home Screen Settings

• Tap the Wallpaper

• Tap the Lock Screen

• Browse through the default options listed in there

- Select one that you like

- If you don't like any of them, tap the More Images option

- Browse through your Samsung Galaxy Note 8 photo gallery

- Select another image, previously downloaded from the web or photographed with your camera app

- Tap the Set Wallpaper button when you're ready.

As you've noticed, the Lock Screen customization options are more than generous. The list of ready to use wallpapers is impressive in itself, not to mention the possibility of adding your own pictures as a background for the Lock Screen!

How to adjust style and font settings on Samsung Galaxy Note 8:

- Start from the main screen

- Access the Notification Shade with one swipe

- Tap on the Settings icon

- Go to the Display section

- Select the Font option

- Browse through all the editing options listed in there;

- Feel free to change the font size, the style, and all the other options provided through the TouchWiz feature.

How to change your ringtones on Samsung Galaxy Note 8:
- Start from the Phone app

- Make your way to the Dialer tab

- From the list of contacts displayed in there, pick one

- You'll see that there will be a pen-shaped icon listed next to that contact name

- Select the editing symbol

- Select the option labeled as Ringtone

- Decide if you want to select a new Ringtone from the list that will extend

- Or browse for a new ringtone, by using the Add button that will take you to the Music folder.

If you've transferred the songs that you'd like to use on your Samsung Galaxy Note 8, there's no reason why you shouldn't be able to select them and configure them as custom ringtones. Speaking of which, the steps described above are for a single contact. If you want to personalize other contacts, just repeat these steps and pick another song. Don't forget you can do the same for the messages notification sounds too!

UNIQUE USES

How to enable the wireless printing on Samsung Galaxy Note 8:

• It all starts from the Settings menu, that you can access either from the Apps tray or from the Notification Shade

• Browse until you find the Connect & Share option

• Tap on it and then tap the Printing button

• Look at the list of pre-installed printers and see if you can find yours

- If your printer is not listed in there, use the Plus symbol to get to the Play Store and select your printer brand in there

- Back to the Printing settings section, you should find its name listed at the Print Enabler option

- Select it only after you have verified that the printer is turned on

- Wait a few seconds for the device to scan, identify, and select your wireless printer

- Now you can start printing documents straight from the phone.

It's a good thing that your Android software now comes with enough information – as in the required software – to be able to print wirelessly, just by simply downloading the specific driver plugin for that printer. From Epson and HP to Lexmark, Brother, or any other wireless printer you can think of, use the instructions from above and get started.

How to connect your Samsung Galaxy Note 8 to the TV, wirelessly:

• Begin by purchasing a Samsung AllShare Hub (in case you don't have a smart TV – if you have one, you can skip this step!)

• Connect the AllShare Hub to the TV with one of those regular HDMI cables

• Connect the AllShare Hub to the local wireless network

• Connect the TV to the same local wireless network

• Now head to the general Settings menu

• Activate the Screen Mirroring option listed in there.

That's it, from this moment, whatever you get to do on the screen of your Samsung Galaxy Note 8 will be automatically displayed on the TV's screen, as long as the screen mirroring option is turned on and the Hub and the TV have access to the same network.

How to use Samsung Galaxy Note 8 as a flashlight

• The first thing you should know is that the flashlight feature is provided by a special widget called Torch

- To access the Torch easily, you will need to bring it to your Home screen or to any of the easily accessible panels, as a shortcut

- Start from the Home screen, where you should long press until the Edit Mode activates

- Select the Widgets option that will be listed towards the end of the screen, next to the Wallpapers and Home Screen Settings

- From the list of widgets, select the Torch

- Hold on its icon and start dragging it to a free position from the Home screen

- When you release it, the icon should permanently remain there.

From now on, to use the Torch app on your Samsung Galaxy Note 8, you will simply have to tap its icon once and it will turn on. Then, you'll tap its icon for the second time and it will turn off. Simple, without any other complications, while it looks like all your other app icons.

How to configure your alarms on Samsung Galaxy Note 8:

- Begin by creating the alarm – go to Apps, select the Clock, and tap the Create option

- Continue to configure the alarm, by tapping the available options, starting with the most important information – like the time – and ending with details like the name of the alarm.

All in all, you have no less than 7 different fields that you can customize. Aside from the two that we just mentioned above, you can select on what days it should repeat, how it should act, what tone to reproduce if you opt for the Sound alarm type, and what volume to have.

Of course, you also have the famous Snooze option, which, in order to be accessible when the alarm rings, it must first be activated from the settings. While you are doing so, select the desired Repeat number (1, 2, 3, 6, 10 times) and the desired interval (3, 6, 10, 16, 30 minutes).

You'll see that, if you want, you can have the alarm to ring only on particular days throughout the week or every single day, Monday to Sunday. You can choose to trigger just the vibration, just the sound, or both of them. And you can pick your favorite song as an alarm tone. It's a lot that you have to tackle, but you'll enjoy it every step of the way.

SPECIAL FEATURES
How to activate text-to-speech on Samsung Galaxy Note 8:

- Go to Settings

- Select the System option

- Access the Language & Input category

- Tap on Speech

- Tap on Text-to-Speech

- Select your preferred TTS engine – you have the Google Text-to-Speech engine and the Samsung Text-to-Speech engine

- Tap the Settings icon associated to the selected TTS

- Choose to Install Voice Data

- Use the Download button and wait to download the language package

- Use the back key when it's done

- Select your language from the list.

Following these steps, the Samsung Galaxy Note 8 will be able to read you various pieces of information out loud. From books to general translations, the read text feature in different languages is a very cool thing to use.

How to turn off the S Voice on your Samsung Galaxy Note 8:
- To disable the S Voice, you will first have to access its main window

- Double tap on the Home button of the device and the S Voice will launch

- Look for the three-dot icon, the symbol of the Settings menu, and tap on it

- From the list that extends, tap on Settings

- From the list of all the options that the S Voice can support, find the Wake-Up section

- Locate the option that enables it to Open Via The Home Key and deactivate it

- From now on, you will no longer accidentally launch the S Voice whenever you tap the Home button.

How to turn on and off the Autocorrect on your Samsung Galaxy Note 8:
- Launch any app with the keyboard option active

- Access the keyboard within that app and select the Dictation Key

- Select the Settings icon

- Select Smart Typing

- In there, tap on Predictive Text and it will automatically switch from On to Off.

This is the simple way to turn off the Autocorrect. As you can imagine, you'll have to do the same when you are trying to turn it back on. The greatest benefit of this action, however, is that it will help you discover other similar functions. Samsung Galaxy Note 8 comes with a pack of helpful features relating to your typing habits. The Auto-capitalization and the punctuation marks may also catch your eye while you're analyzing the Autocorrect options.

How to create a new folder on Samsung Galaxy Note 8

The last thing we would like to show you with this comprehensive guide relates to creating new folders. The more apps you install or the more widgets you bring to the Home screen, the more you will need a way to organize it with new folders. Speaking of which, you can create folders for all your widgets, apps, icons, with the following simple steps:

• Pick the first app that you would place in that folder and select it

• Long press on the app while you drag it at the top of the screen

• Only release the app on top of the New Folder option

• You'll see that the smartphone will ask you to edit the name of the folder that you have just created

• Do that and the small window will disappear

• Now you have a folder on the Home screen, with that first app already inside of it, and you can select, drag, and drop other apps on top of it or just create a new folder from scratch.

HOW TO KEEP A SMARTPHONE FROM BEING HACKED

Even if you keep your smartphone safe in your pocket or purse, it's still at risk for picking up a virus or leaking data to thieves. Hackers don't need physical access to your phone to steal your personal information or infect the device with malware. They infiltrate your phone with innocent-looking apps or link to it via unsecured Wi-Fi networks. You can keep hackers from getting the upper hand by taking steps to secure your smartphone.

Step 1

Lock your phone when you're not using it. Set a password and change it regularly to prevent others from guessing it. Lock patterns are an alternative if you have trouble remembering your password. Your phone may also have a facial-recognition lock feature. If this is on, the device unlocks only when the camera detects your face. Voice recognition is another option; with this turned on, your phone needs to hear your voice say a specific word or phrase to unlock.

Step 2

Activate your phone's tracker capability, if it has one. If your phone supports this feature, you can see its location on a map and track the device when it moves. If your phone is stolen or lost, use the tracker app to lock it remotely. This makes it harder for hackers to access your data.

Step 3

Update your phone's firmware to the most current version. Many phones do this for you automatically, but if you've turned this option off, you'll need to download the update manually. You can download the latest update directly from your phone. Alternatively, connect your phone to the computer and launch the software that came with the device. The application will connect to the download Web page and install the firmware on your phone.

Step 4

Install apps on your phone only if they come from a trusted source, such as the manufacturer's app store. Most official app stores verify the authenticity of their products, so they're much safer. Before downloading any app, read the description and reviews so you understand what you're getting.

Step 5

Check an app's permissions before installing it. If an app reꞩuests access to your personal information, don't install it or deny the request.

Step 6

Avoid leaving your phone alone in a public place, such as on a restaurant table or on your office desk. If you must leave the phone, keep it locked and hide it somewhere, such as in a drawer, to prevent theft.

Step 7

Delete text messages from unknown senders that ask for your information, and avoid clicking links in messages. Some hackers send messages that appear to be from your bank or another trusted source. If you click the link in the message, the hacker can steal your information or install malware on the phone. Don't download apps via text message; this is a common way for hackers to infect your device.

Step 8

Access the Internet on your phone only from a secure Wi-Fi network. Wi-Fi networks that aren't secure allow nearby hackers to intercept your data when you get online. Don't do any shopping or banking on a public Wi-Fi network; hackers can swipe your bank account number or other financial information. Instant-messaging and other communications apps may contain security holes that allow hackers to snatch your personal data. If you have access to a cellular network, use it instead of public Wi-Fi.

Step 9

Protect your phone with an anti-virus app. Check your phone's app store to see what's available for your device.

Tip

Your smartphone may have been hacked if you notice apps opening by themselves or if the battery drains much faster than normal. Unusual charges on your wireless bill also indicate a problem.

CONCLUSION

There is much to like about the Samsung Galaxy Note8; not only does it offer some of the most impressive features in several areas of its spec list, but provides an innovative and appealing introduction to a new platform which bridges the gap between smartphone and tablet.

Ideal for business users, it is also powerful enough to cater to the needs of even the most discerning multimedia user. If versatility is high on your list of priorities when choosing a new smartphone, the Samsung Galaxy Note8 comes highly recommended.

I am extremely glad that you have read the whole book. You have found time in your busy schedule to read this eBook and it means a lot for me. I would like to ask you one final question. Would you please leave a review of this eBook on Amazon in case you like it? I would really appreciate it because nothing is more satisfying for me than helping other people.

Or would you please send me an email in case you do not like this eBook? I would rewrite everything you do not like to make both of us happy. That is all for now. Enjoy the day a have a lot of fun in life!

DISCLAIMER

Although the author and publisher have made every effort to ensure that the information in this book was correct at press time, the author and publisher do not assume and hereby disclaim any liability to any party for any loss, damage, or disruption caused by errors or omissions, whether such errors or omissions result from negligence,

Made in the USA
Columbia, SC
25 November 2017